Level 1
Level 1b

Vocabulary and Grammar
Lesson Review Bookmarks

HOLT McDOUGAL
a division of Houghton Mifflin Harcourt

For more information about this Holt McDougal product,
call 1-800-462-6595, or visit our Web site at: holtmcdougal.com

ISBN13: 978-0-618-79860-5
ISBN10: 0-618-79860-9

291428

Manufactured in the U.S.A. PO # 4500583315

Greet People and Say Goodbye

GREETINGS

Buenos días.	*Good morning.*
Buenas tardes.	*Good afternoon.*
Buenas noches.	*Good evening.*
Hola.	*Hello./Hi.*

SAY GOODBYE

Adiós.	*Goodbye.*
Buenas noches.	*Good night.*
Hasta luego.	*See you later.*
Hasta mañana.	*See you tomorrow.*

SAY HOW YOU ARE

¿Cómo estás?	*How are you? (familiar)*
¿Cómo está usted?	*How are you? (formal)*
¿Qué tal?	*How is it going?*
Bien.	*Fine.*
Mal.	*Bad.*
Más o menos.	*So-so.*
Muy bien.	*Very well.*
Regular.	*Okay.*
¿Y tú?	*And you? (familiar)*
¿Y usted?	*And you? (formal)*
¿Qué pasa?	*What's up?*

Say Which Day It Is

¿Qué día es hoy?	*What day is today?*
Hoy es...	*Today is...*
Mañana es...	*Tomorrow is*
el día	*day*
hoy	*today*
mañana	*tomorrow*
la semana	*week*

Describe the Weather

¿Qué tiempo hace?	*What is the weather like?*
Hace calor.	*It is hot.*
Hace frío.	*It is cold.*
Hace sol.	*It is sunny.*
Hace viento.	*It is windy.*
Llueve.	*It is raining.*
Nieva.	*It is snowing.*

Say Where You Are From

¿De dónde eres?	*Where are you (familiar) from?*
¿De dónde es?	*Where is he/she from?*
¿De dónde es usted?	*Where are you (formal) from?*
Soy de...	*I am from...*
Es de...	*He/She is from...*

Make Introductions

¿Cómo se llama?	*What's his/her/your (formal) name?*
Se llama...	*His/Her name is...*
¿Cómo te llamas?	*What's your (familiar) name?*
Me llamo...	*My name is...*
Te/Le presento a...	*Let me introduce you (familiar/formal) to...*
El gusto es mío.	*The pleasure is mine.*
Encantado(a).	*Delighted./Pleased to meet you.*
Igualmente.	*Same here./Likewise.*
Mucho gusto.	*Nice to meet you.*
¿Quién es?	*Who is he/she/it?*
Es...	*He/She/It is...*

Exchange Phone Numbers

¿Cuál es tu/su número de teléfono?	*What's your (familiar/ formal) phone number?*
Mi número de teléfono es...	*My phone number is...*

Other Words and Phrases

la clase	*class*
el (la) maestro(a) de español	*Spanish teacher (male/ female)*
Perdón.	*Excuse me.*
el país	*country*
(Muchas) Gracias.	*Thank you (very much).*
el señor (Sr.)	*Mr.*
la señora (Sra.)	*Mrs.*
la señorita (Srta.)	*Miss*
sí	*yes*
no	*no*

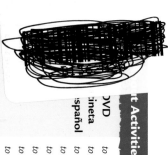

¡Avancemos! Unidad 1, Lección 1
VOCABULARIO

...t Activities

DVD	to rent a DVD
...ineta	to skateboard
...spañol	to learn Spanish
to eat	
to drink	
el jugo	juice...
to buy	
to run	
to rest	
dibujar	to draw
escribir correos electrónicos	to write e-mails
escuchar música	to listen to music
estudiar	to study
hablar por teléfono	to talk on the phone
hacer la tarea	to do homework
jugar al fútbol	to play soccer
leer un libro	to read a book
mirar la televisión	to watch television
montar en bicicleta	to ride a bike
pasar un rato con los amigos	to spend time with friends
pasear	to go for a walk
practicar deportes	to practice / play sports
preparar la comida	to prepare food / a meal
tocar la guitarra	to play the guitar
trabajar	to work

Say What You Like and Don't Like to Do

¿Qué te gusta hacer?	What do you like to do?
¿Te gusta...?	Do you like...?
Me gusta...	I like...
No me gusta...	I don't like...

Snack Foods and Beverages

el agua (fem.)	water
la fruta	fruit
la galleta	cookie
el helado	ice cream
el jugo	juice
las papas fritas	French fries
la pizza	pizza
el refresco	soft drink

Other Words and Phrases

la actividad	activity
antes de	before
después (de)	afterward, after
la escuela	school
más	more
o	or
pero	but
también	also

¡Avancemos! Unidad 1, Lección 2
VOCABULARIO

Describe Yourself and Others

¿Cómo eres?	What are you like?
PERSONALITY	
artístico(a)	artistic
atlético(a)	athletic
bueno(a)	good
cómico(a)	funny
desorganizado(a)	disorganized
estudioso(a)	studious
inteligente	intelligent
malo(a)	bad
organizado(a)	organized
perezoso(a)	lazy
serio(a)	serious
simpático(a)	nice
trabajador(a)	hard-working
APPEARANCE	
alto(a)	tall
bajo(a)	short (height)
bonito(a)	pretty
grande	big, large; great
guapo(a)	good-looking
joven (pl. jóvenes)	young
pelirrojo(a)	red-haired
pequeño(a)	small
viejo(a)	old
Tengo...	I have...
Tiene...	He / She has
pelo rubio	blond hair
pelo castaño	brown hair

People

el (la) amigo (a)	friend
la chica	girl
el chico	boy
el (la) estudiante	student
el hombre	man
la mujer	woman
la persona	person

Other Words and Phrases

muy	very
un poco	a little
porque	because
todos(as)	all

Subject Pronouns and ser

Ser means *to be*. Use **ser** to identify a person or say where he or she is from.

	Singular		Plural	
yo	**soy**	nosotros(as)	**somos**	
tú	**eres**	vosotros(as)	**sois**	
usted	**es**	ustedes	**son**	
él, ella	**es**	ellos(as)	**son**	

Gustar with an Infinitive

Use **gustar** to talk about what people like to do.

A mí **me gusta** dibujar.
A ti **te gusta** dibujar.
A usted **le gusta** dibujar.
A él, ella **le gusta** dibujar.
A nosotros(as) **nos gusta** dibujar.
A vosotros(as) **os gusta** dibujar.
A ustedes **les gusta** dibujar.
A ellos(as) **les gusta** dibujar.

Nota gramatical: Use **de** with the verb **ser** to talk about where someone is from. *Yo* **soy** *de Miami. Ellos* **son** *de California.*

Definite and Indefinite Articles

In Spanish, articles match nouns in gender and number.

		Definite Article	Noun	Indefinite Article	Noun
Masculine	Singular	el	chico	un	chico
	Plural	los	chicos	unos	chicos
Feminine	Singular	la	chica	una	chica
	Plural	las	chicas	unas	chicas

Noun-Adjective Agreement

In Spanish, adjectives match the gender and number of the nouns they describe.

	Singular	Plural
Masculine	el chico alto	los chicos altos
Feminine	la chica alta	las chicas altas

Nota gramatical: Use **ser** to describe what people are like. *Ella* **es** *alta. Mis amigos* **son** *simpáticos.*

Tell Time and Discuss Daily Schedules

¿A qué hora es...?	At what time is . . . ?
¿Qué hora es?	What time is it?
A la(s)...	At . . . o'clock.
Es la... / Son las...	It is . . . o'clock.
de la mañana	in the morning (with a time)
de la tarde	in the afternoon (with a time)
de la noche	at night (with a time)
la hora	hour; time
el horario	schedule
menos	to, before (telling time)
el minuto	minute
...y cuarto	quarter past
...y (diez)	(ten) past
...y media	half past

Describe Classes

Other Words and Phrases

casi	almost
¿Cuántos(as)...?	How many . . . ?
difícil	difficult
en	in
el examen (pl. los exámenes)	exam
fácil	easy
hay...	there is, there are . . .
muchos(as)	many
tarde	late
temprano	early
tener que	to have to

NUMBERS FROM 11 TO 100 p. 87

Describe Frequency

de vez en cuando	once in a while
muchas veces	often, many times
mucho	a lot
nunca	never
siempre	always
todos los días	every day

SCHOOL SUBJECTS

el arte	art
las ciencias	science
el español	Spanish
la historia	history
el inglés	English
las matemáticas	math

CLASSROOM ACTIVITIES

contestar	to answer
enseñar	to teach
llegar	to arrive
necesitar	to need
sacar una buena / mala nota	to get a good / bad grade
tomar apuntes	to take notes
usar la computadora	to use the computer

Describe Classes

aburrido(a)	boring
divertido(a)	fun
interesante	interesting

Describe Classroom Objects

el borrador	eraser
la calculadora	calculator
el cuaderno	notebook
el escritorio	desk
el lápiz (pl. los lápices)	pencil
el mapa	map
la mochila	backpack
el papel	paper
el pizarrón (pl. los pizarrones)	board
la pluma	pen
la puerta	door
el reloj	clock; watch
la silla	chair
la tiza	chalk
la ventana	window

Places in School

el baño	bathroom
la biblioteca	library
la cafetería	cafeteria
el gimnasio	gymnasium
la oficina del (de la) director(a)	principal's office
el pasillo	hall

Say Where Things Are Located

al lado (de)	next to
cerca (de)	near (to)
debajo (de)	underneath, under
delante (de)	in front (of)
dentro (de)	inside (of)
detrás (de)	behind
encima (de)	on top (of)
lejos (de)	far (from)

Other Words and Phrases

¿(A)dónde?	(To) Where?
¿Cuándo?	When?
cuando	when
el problema	problem

Talk about How You Feel

cansado(a)	tired
contento(a)	content, happy
deprimido(a)	depressed
emocionado(a)	excited
enojado(a)	angry
nervioso(a)	nervous
ocupado(a)	busy
tranquilo(a)	calm
triste	sad

The Verb tener

Use the verb **tener** to talk about what you have.

tener *to have*		
yo	**tengo**	nosotros(as)	**tenemos**
tú	**tienes**	vosotros(as)	**tenéis**
usted, él, ella	**tiene**	ustedes, ellos(as)	**tienen**

Tener + **que** + **infinitive** is used to talk about what someone has to do.

Present Tense of –ar Verbs

To form the present tense of a regular verb that ends in **–ar**, drop the **–ar** and add the appropriate ending.

hablar *to talk, to speak*		
yo	**habl**o	nosotros(as)	**habl**amos
tú	**habl**as	vosotros(as)	**habl**áis
usted, él, ella	**habl**a	ustedes, ellos(as)	**habl**an

Nota gramatical: For the numbers 21, 31, and so on, use **veintiún, treinta y un**, and so on before a masculine noun. Use **veintiuna, treinta y una**, and so on before a feminine noun.

The Verb estar

Use **estar** to indicate location and say how people feel.

estar *to be*		
yo	**estoy**	nosotros(as)	**estamos**
tú	**estás**	vosotros(as)	**estáis**
usted, él, ella	**está**	ustedes	**están**
		ellos(as)	**están**

The Verb ir

Use **ir** to talk about where someone is going.

ir *to go*		
yo	**voy**	nosotros(as)	**vamos**
tú	**vas**	vosotros(as)	**vais**
usted, él, ella	**va**	ustedes	**van**
		ellos(as)	**van**

Nota gramatical: To form a question, you can switch the position of the verb and the subject.

Talk About Foods and Beverages

MEALS

el almuerzo	lunch
la bebida	beverage, drink
la cena	dinner
compartir	to share
la comida	food; meal
el desayuno	breakfast
vender	to sell

FOR BREAKFAST

el café	coffee
el cereal	cereal
el huevo	egg
el jugo de naranja	orange juice
la leche	milk
el pan	bread
el yogur	yogurt

FOR LUNCH

la hamburguesa	hamburger
el sándwich de jamón y queso	ham and cheese sandwich
la sopa	soup

FRUIT

la banana	banana
la manzana	apple
las uvas	grapes

Describe Feelings

tener ganas de...	to feel like . . .
tener hambre	to be hungry
tener sed	to be thirsty

Ask Questions

¿Cómo?	How?
¿Cuál?	Which?, What?
¿Por qué?	Why?
¿Qué?	What?
¿Quién?	Who?

Other Words and Phrases

ahora	now
Es importante.	It's important.
horrible	horrible
nutritivo(a)	nutritious
otro(a)	other
para	for; in order to
rico(a)	tasty, delicious

Talk About Family

la abuela	grandmother
el abuelo	grandfather
los abuelos	grandparents
la familia	family
la hermana	sister
el hermano	brother
los hermanos	brothers, brother(s) and sister(s)
la hija	daughter
el hijo	son
los hijos	son(s) and daughter(s), children
la madrastra	stepmother
la madre	mother
el padrastro	stepfather
el padre	father
los padres	parents
el (la) primo(a)	cousin
los primos	cousins
la tía	aunt
el tío	uncle
los tíos	uncles, uncle(s) and aunt(s)

Pets

el (la) gato(a)	cat
el (la) perro(a)	dog

Ask, Tell, and Compare Ages

¿Cuántos años tienes?	How old are you?
Tengo... años.	I am . . . years old.
mayor	older
menor	younger

Give Dates

¿Cuál es la fecha?	What is the date?
Es el... de....	It's the . . . of . . . .
el primero de...	the first of . . .
el cumpleaños	birthday

¡Feliz cumpleaños!

la fecha de nacimiento	Happy birthday! birth date

Other Words and Phrases

vivir	to live
ya	already

NUMBERS FROM 200 TO 1,000,000

doscientos (as)	200
trescientos (as)	300
cuatrocientos (as)	400
mil	1000
un millón (de)	1,000,000

MONTHS

enero	January
febrero	February
marzo	March
abril	April
mayo	May
junio	June
julio	July
agosto	August
septiembre	September
octubre	October
noviembre	November
diciembre	December

Possessive Adjectives

In Spanish, **possessive adjectives** agree in number with the nouns they describe. **Nuestro(a)** and **vuestro(a)** must also agree in gender with the nouns they describe.

Singular Possessive Adjectives		Plural Possessive Adjectives	
mi	**nuestro(a)**	**mis**	**nuestros(as)**
my	*our*	*my*	*our*
tu	**vuestro(a)**	**tus**	**vuestros(as)**
your (familiar)	*your (familiar)*	*your (familiar)*	*your (familiar)*
su	**su**	**sus**	**sus**
your (formal)	*your*	*your (formal)*	*your*
su	**su**	**sus**	**sus**
his, her, its	*his, her, its*	*his, her, its*	*thier*

Comparatives

Use with an adjective to compare two things:

If no adjective, use these phrases.

más... que...

menos... que...

tan... como...

Irregular comparative words.

mayor	**menor**	**mejor**	**peor**
older	*younger*	*better*	*worse*

Nota gramatical: Use **de** and a **noun** to show possesion.
el gato de **Marisa** *Marisa's cat*

Nota gramatical: Use **tener** to talk about how old a person is.
¿Cuantos años **tiene** tu amiga? *How old is your friend?*

Nota gramatical: To give the date, use the phrase: Es el + **number** + de + **month.** Hoy es el **diez** de **diciembre.**
Today is the tenth of December.
Es el **primeiro** de **diciembre.** *It is December first.*

Gustar with Nouns

To talk about the things that people like, use **gustar + noun.**

Singular	Plural
me gusta la sopa	**me gustan** los jugos
te gusta la sopa	**te gustan** los jugos
le gusta la sopa	**le gustan** los jugos
nos gusta la sopa	**nos gustan** los jugos
os gusta la sopa	**os gustan** los jugos
les gusta la sopa	**les gustan** los jugos

Present Tense of –er and –ir Verbs

vender *to sell*		compartir *to share*	
vendo	vendemos	comparto	compartimos
vendes	vendéis	compartes	compartís
vende	venden	comparte	comparten

Nota gramatical: To ask a question, use an interrogative word followed by a conjugated verb.
¿Cómo **está** usted? *How are you?*

Nota gramatical: The verb **hacer** is irregular in the present tense only in the **yo** form (**hago**). In other forms, it follows the pattern for **–er** verbs.

Talk About Shopping

el centro comercial	shopping center, mall
¿Cuánto cuesta(n)?	How much does it (do they) cost?
Cuesta(n)...	It (They) cost...
el dinero	money
el dólar (pl. los dólares)	dollar
el euro	euro
ir de compras	to go shopping
pagar	to pay
el precio	price
la tienda	store

Describe Clothing

la blusa	blouse
los calcetines	socks
la camisa	shirt
la camiseta	T-shirt
la chaqueta	jacket
feo(a)	ugly
el gorro	winter hat
los jeans	jeans
llevar	to wear
nuevo(a)	new
los pantalones	pants
los pantalones cortos	shorts
la ropa	clothing
el sombrero	hat
el vestido	dress
los zapatos	shoes
COLORS	
amarillo(a)	yellow
anaranjado(a)	orange
azul	blue
blanco(a)	white
marrón (pl. marrones)	brown
negro(a)	black
rojo(a)	red
verde	green

Expressions with tener

tener calor	to be hot
tener frío	to be cold
tener razón	to be right
tener suerte	to be lucky

Discuss Seasons

la estación (pl. las estaciones)	season
el invierno	winter
el otoño	autumn, fall
la primavera	spring
el verano	summer

Other Words and Phrases

durante	during
cerrar (ie)	to close
empezar (ie)	to begin
entender (ie)	to understand
pensar (ie)	to think, to plan
preferir (ie)	to prefer
querer (ie)	to want

Describe Places in Town

el café	café
el centro	center, downtown
el cine	movie theater; the movies
el parque	park
el restaurante	restaurant
el teatro	theater

In a Restaurant

el (la) camarero(a)	(food) server
costar (ue)	to cost
la cuenta	bill
de postre	for dessert
el menú	menu
la mesa	table
el plato principal	main course
la propina	tip

ORDERING FROM A MENU

pedir (i)	to order, to ask for
servir (i)	to serve

FOR DINNER

el arroz	rice
el bistec	beef
el brócoli	broccoli
la carne	meat
la ensalada	salad
los frijoles	beans
el pastel	cake
la patata	potato
el pescado	fish
el pollo	chicken
el tomate	tomato
las verduras	vegetables

Describe Events in Town

el concierto	concert
las entradas	tickets
la música rock	rock music
la película	movie
la ventanilla	ticket window

Getting Around Town

a pie	by foot
la calle	street
en autobús	by bus
en coche	by car
encontrar (ue)	to find
tomar	to take

Other Words and Phrases

allí	there
almorzar (ue)	to eat lunch
aquí	here
dormir (ue)	to sleep
el lugar	place
poder (ue)	to be able, can
tal vez	perhaps, maybe
ver	to see
volver (ue)	to return, to come back

Stem-Changing Verbs: e → ie

For **e → ie** stem-changing verbs, the **e** of the stem changes to ie in all forms except **nosotros(as)** and **vosotros(as)**.

querer *to want*	
quiero	queremos
quieres	queréis
quiere	quieren

Direct Object Pronouns

Direct object pronouns can be used to replace **direct object nouns.**

Singular		Plural	
me	*me*	**nos**	*us*
te	*you (familiar)*	**os**	*you (familiar)*
lo	*you (formal), him, it*	**los**	*you, them*
la	*you (formal), her, it*	**las**	*you, them*

Nota gramatical: Use **tener** to form many expressions that in English would use *to be.*
Tengo frío. *I am cold*

Stem-Changing Verbs: o → ue

For **o → ue** stem-changing verbs, the last **o** of the stem changes to ue in all forms except **nosotros(as)** and **vosotros(as).**

poder *to be able, can*	
puedo	podemos
puedes	podéis
puede	pueden

Stem-Changing Verbs: e → i

For **e → i** stem-changing verbs, the last **e** of the stem changes to i in all forms except **nosotros(as)** and **vosotros(as).**

servir *to serve*	
sirvo	servimos
sirves	servís
sirve	sirven

Nota gramatical: **Ver** has an irregular **yo** form in the present tense.
Veo un autobús.

Nota gramatical: Use a form of **ir a** + **infinitive** to talk about what you are going to do.

Describe a House

el apartamento	apartment
el armario	closet; armoire
bajar	to descend
la casa	house
la cocina	kitchen
el comedor	dining room
el cuarto	room; bedroom
la escalera	stairs
ideal	ideal
el jardín (pl. los jardines)	garden
el patio	patio
el piso	floor (of a building)
la planta baja	ground floor
la sala	living room
subir	to go up
el suelo	floor (of a room)

Furniture

la alfombra	rug
la cama	bed
la cómoda	dresser
las cortinas	curtains
el espejo	mirror
la lámpara	lamp
los muebles	furniture
el sillón (pl. los sillones)	armchair
el sofá	sofa, couch

Describe Household Items

la cosa	thing
el disco compacto	compact disc
el lector DVD	DVD player
el radio	radio
el televisor	television set
el tocadiscos compactos	CD player
los videojuegos	video games

Ordinal Numbers

primero(a)	first
segundo(a)	second
tercero(a)	third
cuarto(a)	fourth
quinto(a)	fifth
sexto(a)	sixth
séptimo(a)	seventh
octavo(a)	eighth
noveno(a)	ninth
décimo(a)	tenth

Plan a Party

bailar	to dance
cantar	to sing
celebrar	to celebrate
dar una fiesta	to give a party
las decoraciones	decorations
decorar	to decorate
la fiesta de sorpresa	surprise party
el globo	balloon
los invitados	guests
invitar a	to invite (someone)
salir	to leave, to go out
el secreto	secret
venir	to come

Talk About Chores and Responsibilities

acabar de...	to have just. . . .
ayudar	to help
barrer el suelo	to sweep the floor
cocinar	to cook
cortar el césped	to cut the grass
darle de comer al perro	to feed the dog
deber	should, ought to
hacer la cama	to make the bed
lavar los platos	to wash the dishes
limpiar (la cocina)	to clean the kitchen
limpio(a)	clean
pasar la aspiradora	to vacuum
planchar la ropa	to iron
poner la mesa	to set the table
los quehaceres	chores
sacar la basura	to take out the trash
sucio(a)	dirty

Talk About Gifts

abrir	to open
buscar	to look for
envolver (ue)	to wrap
el papel de regalo	wrapping paper
recibir	to receive
el regalo	gift
traer	to bring

Other Words and Phrases

decir	to say, to tell
hay que	one has to, one must
poner	to put, to place
si	if
todavía	still; yet

Ser or estar

Ser and **estar** both mean *to be*.

Use **ser** to indicate origin.
Use **ser** to describe personal traits and physical characteristics.
Ser is also used to indicate professions.
You also use **ser** to express possession and to give the time and the date.

Use **estar** to indicate location.
Estar is also used to describe conditions, both physical and emotional.

Ordinal Numbers

When used with a noun, an **ordinal number** must agree in number and gender with that noun.

Ordinals are placed before nouns.
Primero and **tercero** drop the **o** before a masculine singular noun.

More Irregular Verbs

Dar, decir, poner, salir, traer, and **venir** are all irregular.

decir *to say, to tell*		venir *to come*	
digo	decimos	vengo	venimos
dices	decís	vienes	venís
dice	dicen	viene	vienen

Some verbs are irregular only in the **yo** form of the present tense.

dar	poner	salir	traer
doy	pongo	salgo	traigo

Affirmative tú Commands

Regular **affirmative tú commands** are the same as the **él/ella** forms in the present tense.

Infinitive	Present Tense	Affirmative tú Command
lavar	(él, ella) lava	¡**Lava** los platos!
barrer	(él, ella) barre	¡**Barre** el suelo!
abrir	(él, ella) abre	¡**Abre** la puerta!

There are irregular **affirmative tú commands.**

decir	hacer	ir	poner	salir	ser	tener	venir
di	haz	ve	pon	sal	sé	ten	ven

Nota gramatical: When you want to say that something has just happened, use the verb **acabar de** + **infinitive.**

Acabamos de comprar el pastel para la fiesta.
We just bought the cake for the party

Sports

el básquetbol	basketball
el béisbol	baseball
el fútbol americano	football
nadar	to swim
la natación	swimming
patinar	to skate
patinar en línea	to in-line skate
el tenis	tennis
el voleibol	volleyball

Locations and People

los aficionados	fans
el (la) atleta	athlete
el campeón (pl. los campeones), la campeona	champion
el campo	field
la cancha	court
el equipo	team
el estadio	stadium
el (la) ganador(a)	winner
el (la) jugador(a)	player
la piscina	pool

Sports Equipment

el bate	bat
el casco	helmet
el guante	glove
los patines en línea	in-line skates
la pelota	ball
la raqueta	racket

Talk About Sports

comprender las reglas	to understand the rules
favorito(a)	favorite
ganar	to win
el partido	game
peligroso(a)	dangerous
perder (ie)	to lose

Talk About Staying Healthy

enfermo(a)	sick
fuerte	strong
herido(a)	hurt
levantar pesas	to lift weights
la salud	health
sano(a)	healthy
PARTS OF THE BODY	
la boca	mouth
el brazo	arm
la cabeza	head
el corazón (pl. los corazones)	heart
el cuerpo	body
el estómago	stomach
la mano	hand
la nariz (pl. las narices)	nose
el ojo	eye
la oreja	ear
el pie	foot
la piel	skin
la pierna	leg
la rodilla	knee
el tobillo	ankle

Outdoor Activities

el bloqueador de sol	sunscreen
bucear	to scuba-dive
caminar	to walk
hacer esquí acuático	to water-ski
el mar	sea
la playa	beach
tomar el sol	to sunbathe

Make Excuses

doler (ue)	to hurt, to ache
Lo siento.	I'm sorry.

Other Words and Phrases

anoche	last night
ayer	yesterday
comenzar (ie)	to begin
terminar	to end
¿Qué hiciste (tú)?	What did you do?
¿Qué hicieron ustedes?	What did you do?

The Verb **jugar**

Jugar is a stem-changing verb in which the **u** changes to ue in all forms except **nosotros(as)** and **vosotros(as)**.

jugar to play	
juego	jugamos
juegas	jugáis
juega	juegan

When you use **jugar** with the name of a sport, use **jugar a** + **sport.**

The Verbs **saber** and **conocer**

Both **saber** and **conocer** mean *to know* and have irregular **yo** forms in the present tense.

saber to know		conocer to know	
sé	sabemos	conozco	conocemos
sabes	sabéis	conoces	conocéis
sabe	saben	conoce	conocen

· Use **saber** to talk about factual information you know. You can also use **saber** + **infinitive** to say that you know how to do something.
· Use **conocer** when you want to say that you are familiar with a person or place. You also use **conocer** to talk about meeting someone for the first time.

Nota gramatical: When a specific person is the direct object of a sentence, use the personal **a** after the verb and before the person.
No conozco **a** Raúl. *I don't know Raúl.*

Preterite of Regular **–ar** Verbs

To form the **preterite** of a regular **–ar** verb, add the appropriate preterite ending to the verb's stem.

nadar to swim	
nadé	nadamos
nadaste	nadasteis
nadó	nadaron

Preterite of **-car, -gar, -zar** Verbs

Regular verbs that end in **-car, -gar, or -zar** have a spelling change in the **yo** form of the preterite.

buscar	**c** becomes → **qu**	(yo) bus**qué**
jugar	**g** becomes —> **gu**	(yo) ju**gué**
almorzar	**z** becomes —> **c**	(yo) almor**cé**

Nota gramatical: To express what hurts, use **doler (ue)** followed by a definite article and a part of the body.
Me **duele la cabeza.** *My head hurts.*

Talk About Technology

la cámara digital	digital camera
conectar a Internet	to connect to the Internet
la dirección electrónica (pl. las direcciones)	e-mail address
estar en línea	to be online
hacer clic en	to click on
el icono	icon
mandar	to send
el mensajero instantáneo	instant messaging
navegar por Internet	to surf the Internet
la pantalla	screen
quemar un disco compacto	to burn a CD
el ratón (pl. los ratones)	mouse
el sitio Web	Web site
el teclado	keyboard
tomar fotos	to take photos

Talk About Events

anteayer	the day before yesterday
el año pasado	last year
entonces	then, so
luego	later, then
más tarde	later on
por fin	finally
la semana pasada	last week

Talk About Negative or Indefinite Situations

algo	something
alguien	someone
algún / alguno(a)	some, any
nada	nothing
nadie	no one, nobody
ni... ni	neither . . . nor
ningún / ninguno(a)	none, not any
o... o	either . . . or
tampoco	neither, not either

At the Amusement Park

los autitos chocadores	bumper cars
el boleto	ticket
la montaña rusa	roller coaster
subir a	to ride
¡Qué divertido!	How fun!
¡Qué miedo!	How scary!
tener miedo	to be afraid
la vuelta al mundo	Ferris wheel

Places of Interest

el acuario	aquarium
la feria	fair
el museo	museum
el parque de diversiones	amusement park
el zoológico	zoo

Make a Phone Call

dejar un mensaje	to leave a message
la llamada	phone call
llamar	to call (by phone)
el teléfono celular	cellular phone

Talk on the Phone

¿Aló?	Hello?
¿Está...?	Is . . . there?
No, no está.	No, he's / she's not.
¿Puedo hablar con...?	May I speak with . . . ?
Un momento.	One moment.

Other Words and Phrases

con	with
el fin de semana	weekend

Extended Invitations

¿Quieres acompañarme a...?	Would you like to come with me to . . . ?
¿Te gustaría...?	Would you like . . . ?
Te invito.	I'll treat you. / I invite you.
ACCEPT	
¡Claro que sí!	Of course!
Me gustaría...	I would like . . .
Sí, me encantaría.	Yes, I would love to.
DECLINE	
¡Qué lástima!	What a shame!

Preterite of Regular –er and –ir Verbs

In the preterite, –er and –ir verb endings are identical.

vender *to sell*		escribir *to write*	
vendí	vendimos	escribí	escribimos
vendiste	vendisteis	escribiste	escribisteis
vendió	vendieron	escribió	escribieron

Affirmative and Negative Words

Affirmative Words		Negative Words	
algo	*something*	**nada**	*nothing*
alguien	*someone*	**nadie**	*no one, nobody*
algún / alguno(a)	*some, any*	**ningún / ninguno(a)**	*none, not any*
o... o	*either... or*	**ni... ni**	*neither... nor*
siempre	*always*	**nunca**	*never*
también	*also*	**tampoco**	*neither, not either*

Alguno(a) and **ninguno(a)** must match the gender of the noun they replace or modify. They have different forms when used before masculine singular nouns.

Nota gramatical: Ningunos(as) is used only with nouns that are not typically singular. No compro **ningunos jeans.** I'm **not** buying any **jeans.**

Preterite of ir, ser, and hacer

Ir, ser, and **hacer** are irregular in the preterite tense. The preterite forms of **ir** and **ser** are exactly the same.

ir *to go* / ser *to be*		hacer *to do, to make*	
fui	fuimos	hice	hicimos
fuiste	fuisteis	hiciste	hicisteis
fue	fueron	hizo	hicieron

Pronouns After Prepositions

Pronouns that follow prepositions are the same as the subject pronouns except mí (**yo**) and ti (**tú**).

Pronouns After Prepositions	
mí	nosotros(as)
ti	vosotros(as)
usted, él, ella	ustedes, ellos(as)

The preposition **con** combines with **mí** and **ti** to form the words **conmigo** and **contigo.**

Nota gramatical: To express *How + adjective*, use Qué + **adjective** in the masculine singular form. Use the feminine form only when a feminine noun is being described. ¡Qué **divertido!** *How fun!*

Talk About a Daily Routine

acostarse (ue)	to go to bed
afeitarse	to shave oneself
bañarse	to take a bath
cepillarse los dientes	to brush one's teeth
despertarse (ie)	to wake up
dormirse (ue)	to fall asleep
ducharse	to take a shower
lavarse	to wash oneself
lavarse la cara	to wash one's face
levantarse	to get up
maquillarse	to put on makeup
peinarse	to comb one's hair
ponerse (la ropa)	to put on (clothes)
secarse	to dry oneself
secarse el pelo	to dry one's hair
vestirse (i)	to get dressed
TALK ABOUT GROOMING	
el cepillo (de dientes)	brush (toothbrush)
el champú	shampoo
el jabón	soap
la pasta de dientes	toothpaste
el peine	comb
el secador de pelo	hair dryer
la toalla	towel

Talk About a Typical Day

generalmente	generally
normalmente	normally
la rutina	routine

Other Words and Phrases

el campo	the country
la ciudad	city
esperar	to wait (for)
hacer un viaje	to take a trip
en avión	by plane
en barco	by boat
en tren	by train
el hotel	hotel
quedarse en	to stay in
las vacaciones	vacation
de vacaciones	on vacation

Talk About Vacation Activities

acampar	to camp
comer al aire libre	to picnic, to eat outside
dar una caminata	to hike
hacer una parrillada	to barbecue
hacer surf de vela	to windsurf
hacer surfing	to surf
montar a caballo	to ride a horse
el tiempo libre	free time

Talk About Buying Souvenirs

barato(a)	inexpensive
la calidad	quality
caro(a)	expensive
demasiado	too much
el mercado	market
el recuerdo	souvenir
JEWELRY AND HANDICRAFTS	
el anillo	ring
el arete	earring
las artesanías	handicrafts
los artículos	goods
de madera	wood
de oro	gold
de plata	silver
la cerámica	ceramics
el collar	necklace
las joyas	jewelry
BARGAINING	
Le dejo... en...	I'll give . . . to you for . . .
Le puedo ofrecer...	I can offer you . . .
¿Me deja ver...?	May I see . . . ?
¡Qué caro(a)!	How expensive!
Quisiera...	I would like . . .
regatear	to bargain

Indicate Position

aquel (aquella)	that (over there)
aquellos(as)	those (over there)
ese(a)	that
esos(as)	those
este(a)	this
estos(as)	these
¿Qué es esto?	What is this?

Reflexive Verbs

Use reflexive pronouns with **reflexive verbs** when the subject in a sentence is the same as its object.

lavarse *to wash oneself*	
me **lavo**	nos **lavamos**
te **lavas**	os **laváis**
se **lava**	se **lavan**

Present Progressive

To form the present progressive in Spanish, use the present tense of **estar** + **present participle.**

-ar verbs	**-er** verbs	**-ir** verbs
caminar ← **ando**	poner ← **iendo**	abrir ← **iendo**
cami**nando**	po**niendo**	ab**riendo**

Some verbs have a spelling change or a stem change in the present participle.

Indirect Object Pronouns

Indirect Object pronouns use the same words as direct object pronouns except for **le** and **les**.

Singular		Plural	
me	*me*	**nos**	*us*
te	*you (familiar)*	**os**	*you (familiar)*
le	*you (formal), him, her*	**les**	*you, them*

Demonstrative Adjective

In Spanish, **demonstrative adjectives** must match the nouns they modify in gender and number.

	Singular	Plural
Masculine	**este** anillo	**estos** anillos
	ese anillo	**esos** anillos
	aquel anillo	**aquellos** anillos
Feminine	**esta** camiseta	**estas** camisetas
	esa camiseta	**esas** camisetas
	aquella camiseta	**aquellas** camisetas